C000179995

# Curiositi.∪υ

## of

# Worcestershire

# Curiosities

## of

# Worcestershire

## A County Guide
## to the Unusual

by

## Ann Moore

S.B. Publications

To my sons, David and Jonathan,
with thanks for their encouragement and practical help

First published in 1991 by S.B. Publications
Unit 2, The Old Station Yard, Pipe Gate, Nr. Market Drayton
Shropshire TF9 4HY

**British Library Cataloguing in Publication Data**
Moore, Ann
    Curiosities of Worcestershire:
    A county guide to the unusual.
    1. Hereford and Worcester (England). Curiosities
    I. Title
    030.94244

    ISBN 1-870708-70-9

Typeset and printed by Delmar Press (Colour Printers) Ltd., Nantwich, Cheshire
Bound by Manchester Free Press, Jersey Street, Manchester M4 6FP

# CONTENTS

# ACKNOWLEDGEMENTS

I must offer thanks to all those who have been so generous in their help: to the National Trust and English Heritage, to the incumbents of the church interiors I have included, to Dame Eanswy of Stanbrook Abbey, Lady Holland Martin, Mr. Parker-Jervis, Mr. Brocklehurst of Sunfield and Mr. Wilton of Spetchley, Mrs. Stone, Mr. Edmondson, Mrs. Popert, Mr and Mrs. Griffiths and Mr. and Mrs. Cox of Harvington Hall among others. In particular, I am indebted to Clive Haynes. He offered his photographic expertise to augment my collection, and, with Gill, was happy to spend some of his spare time driving round the countryside photographing my 'treasures' so that you, too, may enjoy them.

Picture credits: CH — Clive Haynes. All other illustrations photographed by the author.

*Front cover:* Spetchley — The root-house.
*Half-title page:* Head of Oliver Cromwell, Guildhall, Worcester.
*Page 1:* Rous Lench — pillar box.
*Back Cover:* Malvern Priory — misericords.

# WORCESTERSHIRE

The area of the county covers over 700 square miles.

# INTRODUCTION

In this book we explore old Worcestershire. In 1974 boundary changes forced us to think of Herefordshire and Worcestershire as one county. The merger was arrived at for bureaucratic not natural reasons, and to many outside council offices this is still difficult to accept. There still remains a pride and a strong individuality within each separate county and I have reflected this in my search for, and recording of, past and present treasures. Grouping has been arrived at geographically. Using Worcester as a centre, the areas covered radiate out towards each point of the compass. Approximate mileages are given and the maps referred to are the Ordnance Survey Landranger Maps 138, 139 and 150.

The word 'curiosities' is used in its very broadest term. It is not meant to infer that what is listed is in any way odd in a derogatory sense. Rather, my curiosities are things that I have found interesting because they are historically or architecturally unusual, beautiful or rare. I have looked at them either in admiration or with a smile, or have simply asked myself why? In many cases the objects stand testament to man's eccentricity and his desire for immortality. A few of the buildings are follies, those delightful edifices which are there simply because someone felt like creating them, and which were nearly always built by those who had the time, the imagination and the money to indulge in a natural urge to express their own individuality. I have also recorded things that were once part of a way of life, such as dovecotes and barns, clocks, memorials and misericords. These in particular are a great source of information, depicting as they do seasonal beliefs and occupations. Sadly, some previously recorded curiosities have been swept away by those who failed to appreciate their significance. This is particularly sad in the case of follies, for there is little enough opportunity now to enjoy eccentricity for its own sake.

Inevitably, choosing curiosities is an intensely personal thing. What fascinates one may go unnoticed by another, but I hope you will enjoy my collection, and then perhaps go on to find more of your own. If you wish to follow the path I have taken, I ask that you respect both the object and its environment. Many of the curiosities may be viewed comfortably from the road, but some are privately owned. Please respect this privacy. In some cases you will find that churches are locked — a sad but understandable reflection of our age. Keys may generally be obtained nearby.

This book is not a definitive list of the county's curiosities. I would be very interested and pleased to hear from readers who could supply details of other curiosities in the county. If the interest in this book is sufficient, we may be able to produce a second volume. Happy hunting!

*Ann Moore,*
*Worcester*

*In preparation: The Curiosities of Herefordshire.*

## THE AUTHOR

Brought up in the Isle of Man, Ann Moore has lived in Worcester for the past twenty years with her two sons, now grown up. Since illness forced her to retire from teaching three years ago, she has had time to indulge in her hobbies of writing and a study of local history.

# WORCESTER

## WORCESTER CATHEDRAL: MISERRIMUS

The Cathedral has many treasures for the curiosity seeker, but this memorial stone is often missed. Set in the floor by the Miserrimus door in the Cloisters, it is believed to be in memory of Thomas Morris, a minor Canon and Vicar of Claines — a parish outside the city's northern boundary. Morris, who was a fervent supporter of Stuart James II, refused to take the Oath of Supremacy to William III. As a result he was deprived of his living in 1689 and died an unhappy man — thus 'miserrimus', 'most miserable of men'. A small pane in the window to the right of the garden entrance records his burial — his coffin borne by six maidens all in white, wearing red rosettes to his design.

*CH*

2

# WORCESTER

## WORCESTER CATHEDRAL: KING JOHN'S TOMB

Dating back to the beginning of the 13th century, this Purbeck marble tomb is the earliest of all royal effigies. King John, who visited Worcester eleven times, willed that he be buried here between the Saints Wulstan and Oswald, and it is thought that the figure is almost certainly a likeness of the King.

*CH*

## WORCESTER CATHEDRAL: A RARE FISH

The outline of a large sturgeon proudly lifted from the Severn in July 1835 is rarely noticed today. It is carved at the base of the southern wall near the Cathedral Water Gate. Many look up at the flood levels recorded on the wall nearby, but few know to look down behind the gate itself for the outline. The fish, all 94 inches of it, is displayed in the city's Natural History Museum in Foregate Street.

*CH*

# WORCESTER

## A SPIRE WITHOUT A CHURCH

The slender spire built by Nathaniel Wilkinson in 1751, is all that is left of St. Andrew's Church beside the Severn. Since 1947 it has stood alone, and its height of 245½ feet on so small a base (it tapers from 20 feet to a 7-inch diameter at the top), make it quite spectacular. The Glover's Needle as it is known locally, has been repaired several times and these have been occasions for bets and jokes. In 1801 a barber shaved several customers on top of it, while a local china painter decorated a cup while seated up there. In 1870 the repairs themselves were a topic of conversation, for a kite was used to manoeuvre the ropes in to position for the repairer's ascent — yet another landmark with stories to tell.

# WORCESTER

## A BRIDGE WITH A HOLE

This canal bridge near Rainbow Hill to the north of the city, was made to this design to reduce the weight of the brickwork and in the interests of economy. The canal, the Worcester to Birmingham, was completed in 1815. It has five tunnels and fifty-eight locks, making it one of the most heavily locked for its length in the country.

*CH*

# WORCESTER

## HERE'S LOOKING AT YOU

*CH*

The stone face (left) above the entrance to the Guildhall, is that of Cromwell. Nailed by the ears and looking like the devil, he is there to prove that Worcester was ever faithful to the Royalist cause. Above him in Latin is the declaration: 'May the Faithful City ever Flourish'.

The face (top left, opposite page) is thought to be the death mask of William Guise. He was a local tailor who betrayed Royalist plans, thus helping Cromwell take Worcester during the Civil War in 1651. He was later hanged for his treachery and the original stone mask was set in an alley wall off High Street. A copy of the mask may be seen inside the Austin Reed shop opposite the Guildhall; the shop itself being a sensitive conversion of the old Golden Lion Inn.

Little is known about the other three heads. They can be seen on the wall of number 61, Broad Street above what is currently the Heart of England Tourist Office. The roof of the building itself is topped by a dome. It was thought that this might once have been part of a synagogue, but it is unlikely, and the real reason for the unusual design, or for the figure-heads is unknown.

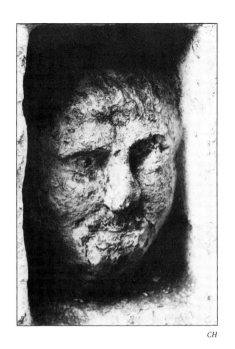

*CH*

*CH*

*CH*

*CH*

7

# BROMSGROVE

## MY ENGINE NOW IS COLD AND STILL . . .

> *Location:* 16 miles north-north-east along the A38.
> *Map Reference:* O.S. map 139 (1:50,000); 957706.

High above Bromsgrove in the churchyard of St. John the Baptist lies the striking memorial to two friends. Thomas Scaife and Joseph Rutherford helped to build a railway and were the first to be killed by it. They joined the Birmingham and Gloucester Railway Company in 1840 as driver and fireman respectively. Together they worked on the formation of the famous Lickey Hills incline, south of Bromsgrove, which had a steep gradient of 1 in 37. By the beginning of November the line finally ran through to Gloucester. When the extension there was opened, Joseph was promoted to foreman of locomotives. Then on 10th November, at teatime, the two men were discussing the day's work in the cab of an engine, aptly named *The Surprise*, as it rested in the station. Suddenly, and without warning, the boiler exploded, hurling Thomas 25 yards away and killing him. Joseph, too, was thrown to the ground and died next day from his injuries and scalding. So these popular young pioneers of steam were laid to rest beside each other, together in death as they had been in life.

Anyone wishing to enter the church may obtain the key from the Rectory.

# BROMSGROVE

## BIG BERTHA

*Big Bertha* was a banking engine specially built for use on the Lickey incline. This 2-mile stretch of line, the steepest on British Rail, with a 1 in 37 gradient, was opened on 17th September 1840. *Big Bertha* helped conquer the early problems of negotiating this rise. A train leaving Bromsgrove was stopped at the foot of the gradient while two engines, known as 'bankers', moved in behind it. They were not coupled to the train. Together they pushed the train before them until it reached the summit, then they dropped back, leaving the train to continue full steam ahead.

The photograph is of a 1:16 model made by Mr. Stubbs and now in safe keeping in Kent.

# CLENT

## A CASTLE FOLLY

*Location:* 27 miles from Worcester off the A491 to Hagley.
*Map Reference:* O.S. map 139 (1:50,000); 924798.

This folly, a listed monument and sometimes known as Clent Castle, lies in 50 acres of parkland at the foot of Adams Hill. It is in the grounds of the Sunfield Children's Home, a residential school for children with severe learning difficulties. To the right of the drive, it stands on a slope partly hidden by trees. There is doubt that it was ever more than it appears today, a two-towered ruin shrouded in mystery; a shelter for the cattle which graze nearby.

*CH*

10

# CLENT

## COAT OF ARMS TO SUNFIELD

The folly is renewed and transformed to silver in the new Coat of Arms granted to Sunfield as recently as October 1990. Designed by Mr. Ralph Brocklebank, Principal of the Home, in celebration of its Diamond Jubilee, it is one of only about 200 Coats of Arms granted each year and is certainly the first to be specifically designed for a Special School. The folly, used here as an heraldic image, stands for the Grail Castle and represents Sunfield's efforts to help each of its children in their search for his or her own Holy Grail.

# HANBURY

## AN ICE HOUSE

*Location:* 12 miles north-east of Worcester, 3 miles north east of Droitwich along a lane leading to the church off the B4090.

*Map Reference:* O.S. map 150 (1:50,000); 945639.

The Ice House at Hanbury Hall, owned by the National Trust, is of mid-18th century construction, a building which at that time was becoming a common feature in most great houses. It would have held about 24 tons of ice, stored there after being cut from a shallow freezing pool, the last in a series of linking pools below the Ice House. The floor of the building, roughly 12ft in diameter, is about 12ft below ground level and the dome is 20ft to its apex. All is neatly bricked and nestling beneath an earth mound. Servants would enter through the 28ft-long passage to collect the ice, which was then carted across the grounds to the Hall. So we see that ice in summer is not the modern luxury that we might think. In fact it is recorded that pits covered with brushwood were used for storing ice by Alexander the Great in the 4th century BC!

*Hanbury — Entrance to the Ice House*

# DROITWICH

## AN ENGLISHMAN'S HOME — CHATEAU IMPNEY

*Location:* 9 miles north-north-east of Worcester along the A38.
*Map Reference:* O.S. map 150 (1:50,000); 915640.

This striking fairytale mansion was built in the 1870s by John Corbett, the Droitwich 'salt king'. Built on the 200-acre site of the manor of Impney, it was designed in the style of Louis XIII by the French architect, Auguste Tronquois who brought over craftsmen from the continent to create the beautiful interior plaster work. The whole is set in well laid out grounds which included fountains, statues, a heated grotto and an ice house. But why did John Corbett want to live in such an ornate 'chateau'? Two theories have been put forward. The romantics believe that John built it to please his wife, Anna Eliza O'Mara, in a vain effort to save a shaky marriage. Others speaking of his rivalry with Sir John Packington, who owned grand Westwood House outside the town, believe the chateau was built as a statement of Corbett's own status. Whichever reason one accepts matters little, for the result is a magnificent building, now an hotel and conference centre.

# ROMSLEY

## IN MEMORY OF A BOY KING

> *Location:* On the B4551, off the A491 to Clent, 1½ miles north-west of the village centre.
>
> *Map Reference:* O.S. map 139 (1:50,000); 945807.

St. Kenelm, whose festival day is 17th July, was, so legend tells us, a 9th-century boy king who was murdered by his sister Quendryth. The ambitious girl was jealous of the wealth and power Kenelm had inherited upon the death of his father St. Kenulf, King of Mercia, in 819 AD. She persuaded her young brother's tutor, Ascebert, to murder the 7-year-old boy and bury his body in a shallow grave. Upon his death, the story goes, a white dove ascended into heaven and when his body was found a spring welled up where he had lain. The water from this spring soon attracted pilgrims, for it was said to have great healing properties, especially in the treatment of sore eyes. An archway in the east wall of the church here at Romsley, led to the spring now known as St. Kenelm's Well.

The spring itself, down a slope beside the church is unprepossessing, but the old mainly Norman building yields items of interest, not the least the carving of Kenelm in the lychgate, and a rare 12th-century tympanum of Christ and two angels above the door.

The key to the church may be obtained nearby.

# DORMSTON

## RARE TUDOR WEATHERINGS

*Location:* 10 miles from Worcester, north of the A422 from Kington, at the
west end of Dormston Village.
*Map Reference:* O.S. map 150 (1:50,000); 984573.

The weatherings round Moat Farm make it one of only two such timber-framed
buildings in the country. Dating back to 1663 or earlier, these rare steeply pitched
tiled awnings are still firmly in place at first and second-floor levels. They were
constructed by Tudor builders to protect the wattle and daub. A solar farmhouse
built round a central hall, Moat Farm was still a working farm until the mid 1980s.
Like the weatherings, the wattle and daub is complete and the house still has the
original staircase, diamond mullioned windows and a star-shaped chimney stack. Moat
Farm is a private residence, although its dovecote facing it across the moat is
maintained by the National Trust.

*CH*

16

# HUDDINGTON

## REMEMBER, REMEMBER . . .

*Location:* 8 miles east of Worcester off the A422 Worcester to Stratford Road.
*Map Reference:* O.S. map 150 (1:50,000); 943537.

Huddington Court is an historic 16th-century timber-framed house, still in private hands, which has been cherished and lovingly maintained through the years. Virtually unchanged, from the moat at its feet to the secret room under the eaves, Huddington was once the home of Thomas Wintour, and if the walls could speak they would whisper of the Gunpowder Plot. Here the brothers Thomas and Robert Wintour discussed the Plot with their cousin Robert Catesby. Here they made final arrangements for the scheme and here they hid after it failed. Because it is a family home, it is not possible to visit the Court, but as you pass to the adjacent church, you may glance across and admire its dignified silence, its well laid out gardens and its fanciful Tudor chimney.

On the wall of the chancel in Huddington's little grey stone church hangs a brass plate engraved with a long ostentatious memorial in Latin. Reading as if it were written by the man himself, it tells of the illustrious life of one Dom Adrian Fortescue. Born in 1601 and 'not content to be distinguished by noble birth merely', he travelled extensively, spoke six languages fluently, 'was learned in philosophy, theology and literature' and finally 'gained such perfection' that he 'won the renown of being . . . worthy of elevation to Heaven'. He died, full of self-satisfaction one feels, on 13th December 1653.

# INKBERROW

## THE OLD BULL

> *Location:* 12 miles east of Worcester on the A422 Worcester to Stratford Road.
> *Map Reference:* O.S. map 150 (1:50,000); 017573.

Since scriptwriter Godfrey Baseley used The Old Bull as a model for his Ambridge pub in The Archers, the hostelry has become something of a curiosity and a mecca for fans of that radio programme. But the Inn itself has always had interesting visitors. Shakespeare is reputed to have stayed here in 1582 on his way to Worcester to collect his marriage certificate (now in the Record Office at St. Helen's in Fish Street, Worcester). Another patron was local curate Edward Pearce. In the early 1600s when it was called The Black Bull, Pearce was a regular customer. In spite of his calling, everyone knew him to be a 'stirrer of strife'. He was seen with another man going 'abroad into the field with two women suspiciously'; and everyone except the Black Bull's hostess doubtless chuckled at the escapade when he had dumped another landlady unceremoniously on the fire after 'watering' the flames in a manner best left to the imagination. Little wonder that in 1602 he appeared at Quarter Sessions to answer charges of 'riotous and lewd behaviour'!

Forty years later customers must also have seen King Charles I when he stayed at the nearby vicarage on the night of 10th May 1645 before the battle of Naseby. There he left, for safe keeping, a book of maps, and details of this treasure may be found in the Church of St. Peter which stands on a rise to the side of The Old Bull.

# SPETCHLEY

## THE ROOT-HOUSE

*Location:* 3 miles east of Worcester on the A422 to Stratford.

*Map Reference:* O.S. map 150 (1:50,000); 896538.

This unusual and enchanting pavilion can be found in the grounds of Spetchley Park, for more than three centuries the home of the Berkeley family. Built in the 18th century and standing about 15ft high and 10ft across, it is made entirely of wood topped with a neat thatch. Eight knobbly trunks of elm form the piers. The walls of hazel coppice, with matching seats, are woven into diamond and diagonal patterns, while beneath the thatch a large elm boss centres an octagonal cone of rough twigs. In two of the walls are small ogee windows which perhaps once held coloured glass. It is thought that this Root-House — one of only three of its type left in England — is modelled on the fronticepiece of *'Universal Architecture',* a book of Arbour designs written by Thomas Wright, an 18th-century architect and astronomer, whose best hermitage can still be found at Badminton.

Spetchley Park Gardens are open occasionally to the public during the summer months.

# FLADBURY

## A GLACIER STONE

*Location:* To the north of Cropthorne between the A44 and B4084 Worcester to Evesham Roads.

*Map Reference:* O.S. map 150 (1:50,000); 995464.

Beside the church wall in the village of Fladbury lies an ancient stone which, millions of years ago began its life in North Wales. Carried down during the glacial period, it is preserved with pride by the parish council as evidence of the extent of the Welsh ice sheet. Another similar stone of Welsh basalt lies south west of Fladbury in Upton on Severn. It was deposited at what is now the corner of School Lane.

# WOOD NORTON

## GATES FIT FOR A KING

*Location:* 4 miles from Evesham on the B4084. Best seen on the right coming from Evesham as one leaves Chadbury.

*Map Reference:* O.S. map 150 (1:50,000); 018470.

Legend says that the handsome wrought iron gates to Wood Norton, now a BBC Engineering Training Centre, originally came from Versailles. In fact they previously fronted York House in Twickenham where Philippe, Duc d'Orleans was born in the middle of the last century. In 1887 the Duc inherited the 4,000 acre Wood Norton estate from his great uncle, son of King Louis Philippe, and the mansion became the centre of a rich and opulent lifestyle where royalty visited regularly. The Duc, an ardent sportsman, had travelled extensively. In the grounds he kept a private zoo and a museum housing souvenirs of his travels — dog kennels which had gone to the Arctic with him, replicas of a cabin in which he had travelled, hunting trophies of lions and crocodiles, pythons and vultures, and an elephant complete with howdah. Now the grand house behind its regal gates, once the home of a would-be king, is used for more mundane purposes and the zoo's polar bear pit is a swimming pool for BBC trainees.

*CH*

# EVESHAM

## A ROUND HOUSE

*Location:* 16 miles south-east of Worcester along the A44 or the B4084.
*Map Reference:* O.S. map 150 (1:50,000); 038438.

Once an inn and also called the Booth Hall, although it was never a 'booth' or market hall, the Tudor Round House has puzzled visitors as to why a building so obviously not round should be so called. The reason is so simple as to be questionable. I am told that it acquired its name because one can so easily walk all round it!

# EVESHAM

## WEATHER-WISE

Those with an anxious eye on
the weather need go no further
than the Town Hall, built about
1580 and known then as New
Hall. Fixed to the wall at the
side of the building is the
barometer, thermometer and
wind indicator clock, presented
to Evesham in November 1887
by the Reverend George Head
of Aston Summerville.

# OFFENHAM

## ONE THATCH OR SEVEN TOGETHER

*Location:* North-east of Evesham off the B4510
*Map Reference:* O.S. map 150 (1:50,000); 054466.

One Thatch can be found in Offenham, a village set among acres of glass-houses in the Vale of Evesham, a sprawl of modern dwellings with its main street set to one side. Main Street is a straight, peaceful 'olde worlde' street with the seven half-timbered cottages nestling together beneath one long thatch. They date from around 1463 and are beautifully trim and neat. At the end of the street is another rarity, a Maypole. This tall red, white and blue pole, topped by a gleaming golden cockerel, has been a permanent fixture since 1987, although traditionally there has been a Maypole on this site for over one hundred years.

# SOUTH LITTLETON

## THE GAZEBO ON A ROOF

*Location:* 6 miles from Evesham on the B4085.
*Map Reference:* O.S. map 150 (1:50,000); 077462.

This striking house, with its unusual chimneys and roof-top gazebo, has an interesting history too long to be written here. With the site of a Roman Road in its grounds, it is almost three houses in one, for the front, brick faced in 1690, leads back into smaller earlier Tudor buildings of local limestone. The 17th-century work was carried out by Francis Taylor, whose initials and the date 1724 can be seen on the weather vane above the central tower. The house is privately owned and therefore not open to visitors, but it can be seen clearly from the church grounds opposite.

# CLEEVE PRIOR

## A GREAT OLD AGE?

*Location:* On the extreme eastern edge of Worcestershire, off the B4085
Evesham to Bidford Road.
*Map Reference:* O.S. map 150 (1:50,000); 088494.

Sarah Charlett's tombstone set to the west of the path of St. Andrew's Church, gives
her age when she died in 1693, as 309. Did the stone-mason leave too great a gap
between the 3 and the 9? Did he seek to fill it with a hyrogliphic? Whatever
happened, the generations remember Sarah for all the wrong reasons although her
family had lived in Cleeve Prior for at least 400 years before her death.

Perhaps great old age is a feature of Cleeve Prior, for the church, found up a side
path off the main road, is shaded by a yew tree reputed to be over 600 years old. On
the external south-west buttress of the tower wall are deep grooves where archers
sharpened their arrows in the Middle Ages. Inside the church are many interesting
historical features including an 8ft. chest probably hewn from the trunk of a single
14th-century elm tree.

# BISHAMPTON

## TO TIME A PARSON

---

*Location:* 6 miles north-east of Pershore off the B4084 through Throckmorton.
*Map Reference:* O.S. map 150 (1:50,000); 990519.

---

In the Church of St. Peter at the northern end of the village, an hourglass stands beside the pulpit; a reminder to a loquacious parson that his sermon should not last too long. The glass itself is a relatively new replacement, made by a visitor to the church, timed to the minute and set into the original old iron stand on the wall. Another such hourglass can be found on one of the benches in the church at Oddingly — this example originally rested in its own free standing iron support, now broken.

# ROUS LENCH

## AN UNUSUAL PILLAR BOX

*Location:* 19 miles from Worcester, south of the A422 Worcester to
Stratford Road.
*Map Reference:* O.S. map 150 (1:50,000); 015533.

Pillar boxes seem to assume some importance in this corner of Worcestershire. Both Rous Lench and nearby Radford boast unusual examples built about 1890 by Dr. Chaffy, a local parson squire. Standing high on their stone plinths, they are like miniature summer houses, each bearing the Chaffy coat of arms beneath its eaves. Going up the shallow steps makes posting a letter an act of some importance! In Rous Lench the box stands beside the Green, across from a striking Grade 2 early Victorian school, now a house, an ornate building of multi-coloured brick with Gothic windows and a bell tower.

# ROUS LENCH

## HALF A YEAR LATER

The unusual half year dating on Lady Rous' tomb can be seen in the annexe within the Church of St. Peter nearby. The memorials there, removed from the chancel walls because they were too heavy, are to members of the Rous family (lords of the manor from 1397 to 1876) who gave their name to this part of the Lenches. Note the beautiful Norman carving of Christ above the tympanium of the church's south doorway.

# WICKHAMFORD

## A TRIPLE-DECKER PULPIT

*Location:* 2 miles from Evesham off the A44 Evesham to Broadway Road, near Badsey Brook.
*Map Reference:* O.S. map 150 (1:50,000); 068424.

Here in the Church of St. John the Baptist one can discover what Pevsner calls 'a real three decker pulpit'. Medieval, and beautifully maintained, it is a rare find in this part of the country. The lowest stall would have been occupied by the Parish Clerk leading the congregation in psalms and responses, while the Minister conducted the service from the middle tier, mounting to the upper pulpit for his sermon.

# WICKHAMFORD

## SALUTATION TO A KING

Above the Chancel arch the Royal Coat of Arms (which may be illuminated by a time switch at the door), has been found to be of more than local interest. During restoration, traces of an older Royal Arms were discovered, possibly dating back to James I, making this painting one of the most interesting in the country.

## THE ORIGINAL STARS AND STRIPES

In a floor-slab memorial behind the altar rails is found what could be called the prototype of the American flag. It is dedicated to a distant relative of George Washington, Penelope Washington who died in 1697. Penelope was the daughter of Colonel Henry Washington who fought for Charles I in Worcester and whose widow at his death married his brother-in-arms, Sir Samuel Sandys. He owned Wickhamford Manor and was a Governor of Evesham during the Civil War. The two bars and three stars were the arms of Penelope's ancestral family.

The key to this beautiful and interesting village church may be obtained from Sir Samuel's old home, the equally lovely Tudor manor house next door.

# ABBOTS MORTON

## THE SMALLEST THATCHED ROOF IN WORCESTERSHIRE

*Location:* 9 miles north of Evesham, west of the A441 Evesham to
Redditch Road.
*Map Reference:* O.S. map 150 (1:50,000); 027550.

*CH*

This delightful pillar box sits beside a cottage restored in 1964 and boasting a straw owl on its own new roof. How nice that the owner thought to thatch the box at the same time. Abbots Morton, a small hamlet hidden away near the Warwickshire border, was once the site of the summer retreat of the Abbots of Evesham. With its simple 14th-century church set on a slight rise at the west end of the street, it still exhudes an air of peace and tranquility.

# BRETFORTON

## WITCHES MARKS

Location: 4 miles east of Evesham off the B4035 to Stratford.
Map Reference: O.S. map 150 (1:50,000); 092437.

These Witches Marks are found in the
Pewter Room and the Brewhouse in the
Fleece Inn (NT) in Bretforton. Circles
have no corners in which evil spirits
may hide, and these were chalked on the
hearth to prevent witches from entering
via the chimney. They have been
renewed so often through the centuries
that in the Brewhouse the stone has
worn away. Other charms protected
doors and windows, and even the cracks
in the flagstones were whitened. In
places these too may be seen in the Inn.
The Fleece was originally a medieval
farmhouse which the family shared with
their animals. It became an inn in 1848,

and it was left to the National Trust, complete with 19th-century family furniture,
by Miss Taplin; the last member of the Byrd family who had lived there for over
500 years.

# BROADWAY TOWER

## A FAMOUS LANDMARK

*Location:* Off the A44 Evesham to Oxford Road, ¾ mile south of Broadway
*Map Reference:* O.S. map 150 (1:50,000); 114362.

No book of this nature would be complete without a picture of Broadway Tower, a much photographed Folly. It is located at the top of Fish Hill, the steep road above Broadway where, legend has it, travellers used to make a will before descending! Perhaps they did this at the old Fish Inn nearby, stopping for a stiff drink and a change of horses before setting off on the perilous journey down into the village. The Inn, originally a summerhouse on the 18th-century estate, has a sundial on its roof.

Standing high on the northern ridge of the Cotswolds, the Tower is a landmark for miles around. 55ft. high and with views over 12 counties from the top, it was

completed in 1797 by the 6th Earl of Coventry, probably to celebrate the centenary of the Earldom. The Earl's family home was the Coventry Estate at Croome d'Abitot and to make sure that his Folly could be seen from Croome Court, about 15 miles away as the crow flies, it is said that a beacon was lit before building began at the point where the tower now stands.

Many famous people have stayed in the tower over the years, not least Sir Thomas Phillips, a great collector of antiquarian manuscripts, who used it to house a printing press, and William Morris who often holidayed here at the end of the 19th century. More recently it was lived in until 1972 by a Mrs. Hutchinson who had been there for 40 years and had brought up a family of three in spite of the bleak and spartan conditions.

Now the tower is at the centre of a lovely country park, open to the public from April to October, and it houses three exhibitions as well as a gift shop.

# FISH HILL

## HOW MANY MILES TO . . .

> *Location:* On the A44 Evesham to Oxford Road at the B4081
> Chipping Camden, Stanway crossroads.
> *Map Reference:* O.S. map 150 (1:50,000).

Strictly speaking this is outside the county boundary, but since it bears the name of the treacherous hill one negotiates to or from Broadway Tower from Worcester it is included. It is easy to miss the tall slim signpost for it stands shaded by a large old spreading beech tree. About ¼ mile away from the top of Fish Hill, going in the direction of Oxford, it stands on the site of an old gallows. With old fashioned finger posts, it points the way in four directions, giving, in roman numerals, the mileage as it was in 1669:

*The way to Oxford*
*XXIIII miles 1669.*

*The way to Warwick*
*XV miles 1669*

*The way to Gloster*
*XVIII miles NI*

*The way to Woster*
*XVI miles NI*

# ST. JOHNS

## A GRAVE PHOTOGRAPH

*Location:* ½ mile from Worcester, on the A4103 to Hereford.

*Map Reference:* O.S. map 150 (1:50,000); 840544.

THE SON OF . HOP INS,
OF THIS CITY, HOP MERCHANT.
JOHN GARMSTON, BORN 1858, DIED 1871.
JONATHAN EDWARD BORN 1868, DIED 1870.

In his posthumous photograph John Garmston Hopkins lies at rest on his shroud in St. Johns churchyard.

Unlike others who keep a picture of a loved one on the mantelpiece, the Hopkins family incorporated their 13-year-old son's photograph into his gravestone and it is still in remarkably good condition after more than 100 years. Anyone looking at the memorial today can understand why it was an idea which has rarely been copied, for the effect is macabre and sends a shiver down one's spine.

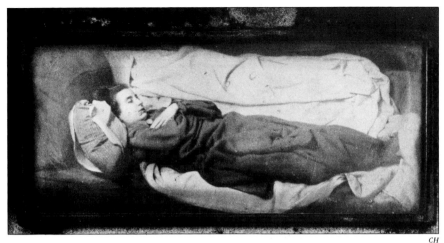

*Close-up of the grave photograph of John Gormston Hopkins*

# ST. JOHNS

## BEHIND THESE WALLS

Still in St. Johns, and about ½ mile further on along the Malvern Road toward the A449 and Powick, one sees Pitmaston School on the right. It lies behind a high solid grey wall topped by small towers, built before the advent of the school, when the house there was privately owned. John Williams (1773-1853), a Tory horticulturalist and County Sheriff, built the wall after the Reform Bill of 1832 "to keep the newly-franchised rag-tag and bobtail out"! It is ironic perhaps that children now play inside his battlements.

# POWICK

## TWO KINDS OF POWER

> *Location:* 2½ miles south of Worcester on the Teme road, off the A449 from Worcester to Malvern.
>
> *Map Reference:* O.S. map 150 (1:50,000); 835525.

This tall chimney at Powick catches the attention of anyone driving between Worcester and Malvern. It is part of the first hydro-electric power station to be built in Europe for public supply. Standing beside the River Teme, it began supplying current in November 1894. It had four turbines with three steam engines capable of working to 286 hp so the generators could be powered by the water turbines or the steam engines or both. It began by supplying power to 181 consumers and 27 street lamps and continued, growing all the while, until the steam plant closed down in the late 1920s. The hydro-electric section continued until 1950 when the generating machinery was removed.

*CH*

The station stands adjacent to Old Powick Bridge, the scene of the first and last battles of the Civil War — 23rd September 1642 when Prince Rupert's men routed a part of Cromwell's men, and 3rd September 1651 when the Royalists under Montgomery held the bridge for two hours until they were cut off. Powick Church of St. Peter, off the B4424 nearby, bears witness to these skirmishes. There are marks on the tower where musket shot hit the stonework as Cromwell's troops advanced toward Powick from Upton on Severn. The new Powick Bridge, in constant use today, was built in 1837. Of cast iron, it was designed with sandstone arches and abutments in a style to match its old counterpart 100 yards upstream.

# CALLOW END

## THE ABBEY CLOCK THAT PINGS

*Location:* 4 miles south of Worcester on the B4424 Powick to Upton Road.
*Map Reference:* O.S. map 150 (1:50,000); 835499.

Peter, Mary Minor and Benedict help the nuns in their enclosed order at Stanbrook Abbey keep time. They are the names of three of the eight bells in the church tower, and they ring not only at every quarter hour, but also at seven minutes before each quarter! Peter rings the hours, while the other two ring the quarters and Mary Minor is responsible for the unusual extra chime, known to the nuns as 'the ping'. These Whitechapel bells were placed, with the clock made by Gillett and Bland of Croydon in 1870, in an equally unusual tower. Made of alternating 'stripes' of brick and stone, the tower was built by Edward Pugin, his design being inspired by a church which he saw from a train as he was travelling through Normandy.

The Tower may be seen from the road, set in the Abbey grounds, on the right as one enters Callow End travelling from Powick.

# EARLS CROOME

## GATEWAY TO OPULENCE

*Location:* 15 miles south of Worcester via the A38 through Kempsey, turning off at Severn Stoke.
*Map Reference:* O.S. map 150 (1:50,000); 888445.

These imposing entrance gates lead into Croome Court, seat of the Earls of Coventry. Built in 1750, the Court was sold by the Coventry family in 1948, and has since been a school and a centre for the Hari Krishna sect. Now in private hands, it is not at the time of writing open to visitors, although the mansion itself can be clearly seen across its grounds from the road.

The very extensive parklands were landscaped by 'Capability Brown' and were said to have 'more park furnishings than any in England' (Pevsner). These, mostly neglected now, included a grotto, dry-arch bridge, temple, sham castle and a lakeside summerhouse with Corinthian columns.

*Croome Court — The 'Panorama'*

The round-domed 'Panorama' Tower was designed by Robert Adam, as were many of the garden 'furnishings'. It stands on a rise, separated from its own home grounds by a busy motor-way.

# RIPPLE

## ST. MARY'S CHURCH: MISERICORDS

*Location:* 13 miles south of Worcester 5 miles north-west of Tewkesbury.
*Map Reference:* O.S. map 150 (1:50,000); 877378.

The misericords in St. Mary's Church, Ripple, are splendid examples of 15th-century craftsmanship. The two illustrated are part of a series of 12 depicting the seasonal occupations of country life, each full of detail and beautifully carved, (see also Malvern page 82).

The church also houses other items of interest, including a rare 'She' Bible of 1613, so called because it had the correct version of Ruth III v 15 — 'and She went into a city . . .' The previous 1611 edition contained the error 'and He went into . . .' Outside, the porch contains a small lepers' trough, once sited near the Cross in the village, while nearby the buttresses bear the scars of sythes sharpened on their corners.

*Misericord detail: March — sowing*

*Misericord detail: August — reaping*

# RIPPLE

## THE GIANT'S GRAVE

CH

*The Giant's Grave*

In the churchyard to the right of the path, is the Giant's Grave. Here lies buried Robert Reeve. Said to be 7 feet 4 inches tall, he died in 1626, aged 56, after taking on a bet to mow the 100-acre Uckinghall Meadow. He leaves this advice for posterity:

> *Ye who pass by behold my length,*
> *But never glory in your strength.*

Away from the church, beside the tiny village green, can be seen rare stocks and a whipping post near the remains of a 14th-century cross, standing at the meeting place of two pre-Roman tracks.

# BREDON

## FIGURES ON A ROOF

*Location:* On the southern edge of Bredon Hill, 17 miles south of Worcester,
   3 miles north-east of Tewkesbury, just north of the B4080.
*Map Reference:* O.S. map 150 (1:50,000); 920370.

These small quaint stone figures can just be seen on top of the old Rectory roof to
the north of St. Giles Church, Bredon. They represent Oliver Cromwell and Charles
II, and it is said that if they ever move from each end of the roof to come together
in the centre, man will see the end of the world!

*CH*

The visitor is drawn to the church by its graceful 14th-century spire. 161 feet high and
slender, it is an unusual feature in a Worcestershire country church. The building itself is
spacious and well maintained, with well documented literature for those interested in its
memorials and church history.

Nearby is Bredon Tythe Barn. Maintained by the National Trust, it is one of the largest in
England and has a Bailiff's solar room over one of its porches, reached by external
stone steps.

CH

*Bredon: Roof detail — Charles II*

CH

*Bredon: Roof detail — Cromwell*

# UPTON ON SEVERN

## THE PEPPERPOT AND CLOSED WINDOWS

*Location:* 11 miles south of Worcester on the A4104.
*Map Reference:* O.S. map 150 (1:50,000); 852406.

CH

No-one can fail to miss Upton-on-Severn's striking landmark, known locally as 'the Pepperpot'. The tower is all that is left of the medieval church of St. Peter and St. Paul which was the first centre of action during the Civil War when it was held by Commonwealth troops against the Royalists, and was then partially rebuilt in the middle of the 18th century. At that time the unstable spire was replaced by this hexagonal wooden lantern and the cupola — the top of the pepperpot. The lead cupola, designed by Anthony Keck, a leading Midland architect, was subsequently sheathed in copper. The church itself was finally pulled down in 1937, leaving the tower to stand alone.

Looking across from the tower, one sees a row of terraced houses. Numbers 2, 4 and 6 are not all that they may seem. Close examination of the upper floor windows shows that they are blocked in. The windows and the brick facade were built to give a more uniform and fashionable appearance to the timber-framed buildings behind.

# KEMERTON

## BELL'S CASTLE

*Location:* 14 miles south of Pershore via Kenerton, off the B4080.
*Map Reference:* O.S. map 150 (1:50,000); 853406.

Bell's Castle is a folly halfway up Bredon Hill, a private home and therefore not open to the public. Complete with battlements and lancet windows, all slightly different, it was built on to existing cottages in 1820 by one Captain Bell, a smuggler. Unfortunately it proved to be an expensive undertaking and so he was forced to return to sea. When he finally came home again he brought back with him, so the story goes, two French ladies of noble birth. It was not long, however, before his nefarious deeds caught up with him. He was betrayed, and hanged in 1841. An illegitimate daughter from Cheltenham took his body and made arrangements for him to be buried at Pershore Abbey — a conventional end to what must have been a very colourful life.

*CH*

47

# KEMERTON

## PARSON'S FOLLY

*Location:* 7 miles south of Pershore off the A44, via Great Comberton,
  then on foot.
*Map Reference:* O.S. map 150 (1:50,000); 957402.

Parson's Folly stands on the highest point of Bredon Hill. It is situated inside the
2,000-year-old Iron Age Hill Fort, a solid grey square tower built in the 18th century
by a Mr. Parsons of Kemerton. Also known locally as 'the summer house', it is now
adorned by various modern aerials, but it may be visited by anyone with energy
enough to make the climb.

*CH*

# KEMERTON

## THE BANBURY STONE (THE ELEPHANT STONE)

*Location:* 7 miles south of Pershore off the A44, via Great Comberton, then on foot.

*Map Reference:* O.S. map 150 (1:50,000); 957402.

The Banbury Stone is very ancient and stands near Parson's Folly on the outer rim of the hill fort. Known to many as the 'elephant stone', it overbalanced from its original standing position about a hundred years ago and broke in to several pieces, so that from a certain angle it does indeed look like an elephant on its knees. In the past, it was an old custom to go to the hill on Good Friday to kiss the stone — for good luck presumably. It is also said that when the bells of Pershore Abbey ring loudly enough for the stone to hear them, it will descend the hill to drink from the Avon.

*CH*

49

# ELMLEY CASTLE

## WHAT'S THE TIME?

*Location:* 13 miles south-east of Worcester off the A44 through Pershore.
*Map Reference:* O.S. map 150 (1:50,000); 982411.

Two sundials in the pretty village of Elmley Castle, nestling at the foot of Bredon Hill, were once believed to indicate the time in any part of the Old World. Since they probably date from the mid-16th century, perhaps Elizabeth I consulted them when she stayed here one late August weekend in 1575. Built of stone and about 22-inches square, the sundials are in front of St. Mary's Church. Each bears several gnomons on all sides, the working edges pointing to the celestial North Pole. It has been estimated that, apart from October and November, the dials now show Elmley Castle time to be 8 minutes behind GMT — testament indeed to the skill and accuracy of the original 16th-century designer.

# ELMLEY CASTLE

## A MEDIEVAL RABBIT

The carving of a rabbit, which greets the visitor when entering the church porch (it is to the right of the door), dates from the middle ages. Facing the rabbit is a carving of a pig of the same age. There is interesting literature within this gracious church to guide the visitor through the many memorials to its history, and also a model of the vanished castle which gave the village its name.

# LITTLE COMBERTON

## MARKS FOR THE FUTURE

*Location:* 4 miles south of the A44 Worcester to Evesham Road.
*Map Reference:* O.S. map 150 (1:50,000); 967427.

It would seem that hundreds of years ago some people in Little Comberton were more than anxious to leave their marks. The stonemason who built the porch of St. Paul's Church in 1639 carved AΓEP to the left of the door. Perhaps he was hoping that his work might last for ever, for it is thought that the letters are Greek or Latin — the Latin being an abbreviated form of AGERATUM which means 'not growing old'.

Inside the porch, cut into one stone bench, are several flat outlines of hands. Dating back to the early 18th century, these are reputed to be the hands of newly married brides. One, perhaps too large to be that of a woman, bears the initials WD; the same letters appearing nearby on a shield dated 1733. One cannot help but wonder who this mysterious WD was.

# LITTLE COMBERTON

## A DOVECOTE

A few hundred yards away from the church, going towards Pershore, is a privately owned circular dovecote at Nash's Farm. Built of stone and in pristine condition, the dovecote shows a different design from that which is usually found (see the illustration of the dovecote at Wichenford page 59). Reputed to be 100 years older than the house, which was built in 1527, the dovecote has 751 nesting boxes and is currently the residence of 35 elegant white doves.

To see England's largest dovecote, one must visit Great Comberton nearby.

*CH*

# BESFORD

## FOR THE LOVE OF A CHILD

*Location:* 2 miles south-west of Pershore off the A4104.
*Map Reference:* O.S. map 150 (1:50,000); 911448.

Besford's 14th-century church of St. Peter, the only timber-framed church in
Worcestershire, has many interesting features, one of the more striking being a large
triptych on the south wall of the nave. Its heavy decorated wings open to reveal
faded paintings and verses lamenting the death of Richard Harewell who died in
1576 at the age of 15, one of three Harewell sons who all died in childhood. His
effigy in alabaster lies on a splendid tomb in the chancel.

Other items of historical interest are the rare pre-Reformation Rood Screen carved
with roses and quatrefoils — there are few left in England now — and the funeral
armour of Sir Thomas Sebright who was buried in 1702. His gauntlets, helmet and
sword still hang near the chancel.

The key may be obtained from the house across the lawn adjacent to the church.

*Besford — 16th-century Triptych*

On the left wing of the triptych, the first four lines read:

> 'Poore childe to whome should I complaine
> In this my grief and mazed plight
> Tyme bends his sythe to cut my threede
> Death waves his dreadfull darre\* i sight . . .'

                         \* dagger

# PIRTON

## PASSPORT TO A SHRINE

> *Location:* 6 miles from Worcester along the A38 through Kempsey,
>    turning off at Severn Stoke.
> *Map Reference:* O.S. map 150 (1:50,000); 886469.

The unique Pirton Stone in St. Peter's Church is a 13th-century ampulla mould which was discovered in 1871 during the rebuilding of the chancel arch. Measuring 12.2 x 9.7 x 3.2 cm, it is of fine-grained limestone and bears a cruciform with figures of the crucifixion, a bishop and a cathedral (possibly Canterbury) on one face. It is believed to be the mould for casting medieval certificates for travellers making the pilgrimage to the shrine of Thomas Hughbeckett. No other examples like this have ever been found. It is now on permanent loan in the Ashmolean Museum in Oxford, but photographs and details are on display in the church.

*Pirton — St. Peter's Church*

# DEFFORD

## DUNSTALL CASTLE

*Location:* 2½ miles from Upton east-north-east of Earls Croome
off the A4104 Upton to Defford Road.
*Map Reference:* O.S. map 150 (1:50,000); 884428.

This splendid piece of eccentricity stands proudly on the edge of rolling fields, impervious to the constant frenetic roar of a nearby motorway. Thought to be one of the Croome Follies, it was designed by Sanderson Miller (1717-1780) who also built Hagley Hall for the 1st Lord Lyttleton. A mock ruin of towers and hollow walls in rough pale stone, the 'castle' is the product of one man's dream, exhuding a strength and permanence which its mortal creator did not have. Like something from a fairytale, one cannot help but wish that it might stand for ever.

# WICHENFORD

## ENGLAND'S LARGEST DOVECOTE

*Location:* 5 miles north-west of Worcester, north of the B4204.
*Map Reference:* O.S. map 150 (1:50,000); 787598.

This dovecote is included as an example of one of the few now existing in such good condition. Owned by the National Trust, and having 557 nesting holes, it is 17th century, timber-framed and in-filled with wattle and daub. Originally built for strictly utilitarian purposes, it is recorded that in 1659 there were 26,000 dovecotes in England. Only the Lord of the Manor had the right to build one and to kill the birds it housed for use in his kitchen; a constant source of anger to often hungry peasants whose crops fell victim to these greedy birds.

(See also Little Comberton, Dormston, Huddington Court.)

*CH*

# CLIFTON-ON-TEME

## THREE UNUSUAL MEMORIALS

*Location:* 11 miles north-west of Worcester, 9 miles from Tenbury on the
   B4204 road.
*Map Reference:* O.S. map 150 (1:50,000); 616714.

*CH*

Clifton-on-Teme is a pretty
village, misnamed perhaps, for
it stands 600 ft. above the river
Teme which is never nearer
than a mile away. As so often
happens, the church here (one
of eight in England dedicated
to St. Kenelm) holds secrets
and stories of the people who
once lived close by.

Opening the very heavy door
with its huge iron hinges and
the largest drop handle in
Hereford and Worcester, the
visitor will encounter the grave
of Elizabeth Taylor, Gent. who
'Lived and dyed A Virgin'.

# CLIFTON-ON-TEME

## THREE UNUSUAL MEMORIALS

Pause then to wonder, too, what happiness, if any, was enjoyed by Elizabeth Hartright, a glover's wife, who died when only 28 after a life 'much Alloy'd with Pains'. Was she consumptive perhaps? Her oval memorial is near a larger ornate marble tablet on the north wall. This must have been carved, one feels, by a weary stone-mason. What other reason could there be for young William dying 9 months before he was born?

As you leave the church notice the recess in the base of the churchyard cross. It is rare to find in such good order, this space designed to hold the pyx used in long ago Palm Sunday processions.

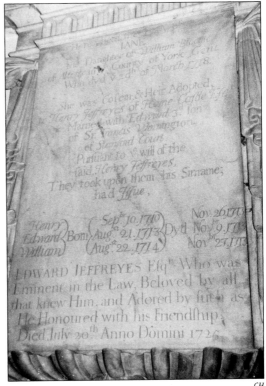

CH

# MARTLEY

## A MEDIEVAL DRAGON

*Location:* 7 miles north-west of Worcester off the B4204.
*Map Reference:* O.S. map 150 (1:50,000); 756559.

This little Welsh dragon puffing his way across rich folds of fabric, is a member of a group of medieval wall paintings said to be one of the best examples of its type in the country. In the lofty red sandstone church of St. Peter, the chancel is covered with 13th- and 15th-century painted pictures — patterned curtains with symbolic medieval animals in the swags, a woman praying, the Annunciation and the Visit of the Magi — all beautifully preserved. Beneath them nearby, lies the effigy of a Yorkist knight, clad in 15th-century armour, his head on his tilting helmet. As you enter the church, you are met by the more modern, almost lifesize, figure of Christ, carved from a single tree trunk.

*CH*

# SHELSEY WALSH

## A PLACE OF REFUGE

*Location:* 11 miles north-west of Worcester off the B4204.
*Map Reference:* O.S. map 150 (1:50,000); 723625.

Dating from the 12th century, the church of St. Andrew at Shelsey Walsh (an area more often remembered for its car hill climbs), has been included for those who appreciate unusual church architecture and design. A tiny church, standing on a rise near Court House (once home of Sir Richard Walsh, Sheriff of Worcester, who helped capture the conspirators in the Gunpowder Plot), St. Andrew's contains a beautiful 15th-century rood beam and screen. The beam beneath its roof of painted stars, is richly carved, and the screen is unusual in that it is returned into the nave so as to enclose a small chantry chapel. There is only one other example of this in England, and that is at Fenney Bentley in Derbyshire.

A recess in the stonework inside the door is a reminder that in times of religious strife churches were places of refuge for fugitives. This recess would have housed a stout oak beam which could be pulled out and shot across the door into another recess, thereby making it impossible to open the door from outside.

In the chancel lies a unique wooden panelled tomb, without effigy, the resting place of Sir Frances Walsh, father of the already mentioned Sheriff.

*CH*

# KYRE WYARD

## A COVERED WAY TO CHURCH

*Location:* 4 miles from Tenbury, off the B4214 Tenbury to Bromyard Road.
*Map Reference:* O.S. map 150 (1:50,000); 636627.

This covered way leading from the house directly to the church is one unusual feature of the church of St. Mary at Kyre Wyard. It could be said that it is in fact two churches in one, for the Squire's Chapel abuts the church and can be entered through a door from the main building. In this small, high windowed and presently dank chapel, is an odd collection, including a faded wall painting, a 17th-century bier and a cannon ball. In the church itself, safely housed in a glass case, there is a rare 1583 Bible, illustrated with charming woodcuts and famous for its mistakes — although as the Bible is placed we cannot see them. In this edition Abilemech's head is spoken of as his 'brain pan', and in the Garden of Eden, we are told, Adam and Eve made 'breeches' for themselves!

It is to be hoped that money can indeed be found to enable the realisation of current plans to renovate this little village church. It would be a pity if it were to join the list of other sad 'redundant' churches in the county. The key may be obtained from the house nearby.

# TENBURY WELLS

## THE SPA THAT NEVER WAS

*Location:* 21 miles north-west of Worcester on the B4204.
*Map Reference:* O.S. map 150 (1:50,000); 679595.

At one time an important coaching town between London and Worcester, Tenbury Wells had great aspirations to become a spa town. Mineral waters were found there in 1839 and a Pump Room and Baths were built at the rear of what is now the Crow Hotel. It was advertised as 'a spa for middling and working classes', offering 'every convenience at the lowest possible price'. The Baths were housed in a decorated conservatory with a tower in the shape of a pagoda. The photograph shows all that is left of what must have been a striking and unusual building looking, as it did then, like several galvanised iron umbrellas collapsing on top of each other. The business never materialised, and soon, no doubt, all traces of these ambitions will be lost for ever.

# TENBURY WELLS

## THE MARKET HOUSE

Standing the test of time far more successfully is the old Market House in the Square, traffic swirling round it on all sides. Built in 1811, this curious oval-shaped building was used as a corn and butter market.

For those interested in exploring churches, St. Mary's near the Market House is worth visiting. Practically demolished in the 18th century by the flooding Teme nearby, it contains, among other items, the fine alabaster tomb of Sir Thomas Acton, whose son-in-law prosecuted Shakespeare for deer stealing and was, it is thought, the model for Justice Shallow. Nearby are two ancient stone Crusaders, one practically life-size and the other only about 30 inches long but with remarkably detailed dress.

# ABBERLEY

## A LANDMARK TO TIME

*Location:* 14 miles north-north-west of Worcester off the A443.
*Map Reference:* O.S. map 150 (1:50,000); 748668.

Abberley clock tower, to some Jones's folly, stands high in the grounds of Abberley Hall, its Gothic pinnacles a landmark for miles around. It was designed as a bell-tower by J. P. St. Aubyn, a Victorian church architect, and built by John Joseph Jones whose wife, Sarah Amelia (Amy), laid the foundation stone on 4th May 1883. Jones had come from Manchester where his family had made money in the cotton industry. There is some suggestion that it is not a memorial to Jones's father or a building to spite nearby Witley Court, but a reminder to his workers that time must not be wasted! For beneath the clock-face is a sundial. Was this there as a double check on precious time, or an insurance against the clock stopping? In time the 20 bells in the clock-tower, which could play 40 tunes, were sold to keep up the Hall. This is now a private school for boys, boasting among its former pupils Sir Geoffrey Howe and the actor, the late Sir Anthony Quayle.

*CH*

# GREAT WITLEY

## PERSEUS AND ANDROMEDA

*Location:* 12 miles north-west of Worcester, ½ mile south of the A443
      Worcester to Tenbury Road.
*Map Reference:* O.S. map 150 (1:50,000); 767648.

This magnificent fountain in the grounds of Witley Court, devastated by fire in
1937, is said to be the largest in the British Isles. Perseus and Andromeda, designed
by James Forsyth (1833-1915) and inspired by Bernini's fountains in Rome, rises 26ft.
above its water level. It is said that beneath it there was a high domed chamber large
enough to hold 50 people, which could be reached through a tunnel from the house.
Protected now by English Heritage, it is to be hoped that one day the fountain
might operate again.

Nearby is the equally magnificent Great Witley Church. Said to be the finest
Baroque church in England, it contains beautiful stained glass windows and ceiling
paintings by the 17th-century artist Antonio Bellucci.

*CH*

# OMBERSLEY

## A RARE PLAGUE STONE

*Location:* 8 miles north of Worcester off the A449.
*Map Reference:* O.S. map 150 (1:50,000); 845637.

The Plague Stone sits, like a large shallow drinking trough, on a small green near the crossroads in the pretty village of Ombersley. A rare item, it originally stood on the Old Packhorse Road near Ombersley Court. There in 1348 at the time of the Black Death, it gathered food for the beleaguered inhabitants from well-wishers, and served to warn travellers to keep away from the village when sickness was rife.

# OMBERSLEY

## THE SANDYS FAMILY PEW

*Location:* 8 miles north of Worcester off the A449.
*Map Reference:* O.S. map 150 (1:50,000); 845637.

The Sandys family pew beside the pulpit in Ombersley church, built in 1825 by Thomas Rickman, has been likened to a little George IV boudoir. Large and square and complete with comfortable cushioned seats and matching blue embroidered kneelers, it boasts an ornate open fireplace in one corner. In the old days members of the Squire's family could avoid all contact with the congregation if they wished, for the pew was curtained and could be reached through a private exterior door beside the altar.

# OMBERSLEY

## THE HOWDEN HEATING STOVE

*Location:* 8 miles north of Worcester off the A449.
*Map Reference:* O.S. map 150 (1:50,000); 845637.

The Howden heating stove against the north wall doubtless provided the rest of the congregation with much needed warmth and probably choking fumes as well. Installed in 1829, it is a 12 ft-high miniature church tower in wrought iron, complete with buttresses, an arcaded top and a narrow fuel door like a church doorway.

It is no longer used for heating the church.

# ARELEY KINGS

## WALNUTS AND A WALL

*Location:* 10 miles from Worcester along the A443 to Holt Fleet,
then the B4196.
*Map Reference:* O.S. map 138 (1:50,000); 802712.

CH

This stone wall forming part of the boundary fence for the church of St. Bartholomew is
not all that it may seem. It is in fact a memorial, placed there at the wish of Sir
Harry Coningsby, a 17th-century Squire who died in 1701. Sir Harry had died an
unhappy man, heartbroken after the accidental death of his son who had drowned
while playing with his father. Sir Harry's epitaph, barely legible now but originally
inscribed on the wall, consisted of five words — one Greek, two Latin and two
English:

> *Lithologema Quare, / Reponitur Sir Harry.*
> *Stone building, why? / Here lies Sir Harry.*

Nearby Sir Harry had planted three walnut trees to provide nuts for the village children,
and he intended that they should use the wall on one day each year to crack the nuts. He
might perhaps be pleased to see these modern children beside his wall, although the
walnut trees are no longer there.

Inside the church beside the Chancel lies another strange, now faded, inscription. It is to
William Walsh 'ruinated by three Quakers, three lawyers and a fanatick to help them',
but his story has been lost in the mists of time. The key may be obtained from the
Rectory adjacent to the church.

# WOLVERLEY

## A HOME IN VALES ROCK

*Location:* 3 miles north of Kidderminster off the A442 to Bridgnorth, on the
 B4189 north of Drakelow.

*Map Reference:* O.S. map 138 (1:50,000); 826821.

This hermitage on the north-west boundary of the county stands about 80ft. above
ground level. Reached by a steep overgrown path, it is a series of interconnecting
chambers cut into an outcrop of soft sandstone during the Industrial Revolution.
Some of the chambers have fireplaces and blackened chimneys, and in places the rock
ceilings have flaked away to show their own beautiful patterns. Vales Rock, unused
since the early 1960s, originally provided accommodation for workers in the iron
factories.

*CH*

73

# WOLVERLEY

## A KNIGHT'S STORY

*Location:* 3 miles north of Kidderminster off the A442 to Bridgnorth, on the B4189 north of Drakelow.

*Map Reference:* O.S. map 138 (1:50,000); 829792.

Wolverley Church, too, stands in a commanding position above the village on another escarpment of red sandstone. Built of red brick, it guards the 14th-century effigy of Sir John Attwood, a knight about whom there is an interesting legend.

Sir John, while following the Black Prince on a Crusade in the Holy Land, was captured by the Saracens and thrown into a dungeon. His unhappy lady, waiting in vain for his return to Wolverley Hall, finally gave him up for dead. She was about to remarry, when a frightened maidservant rushed in with news of a dying stranger in the meadows. It was the family's dog which recognised that the stranger was Sir John, who had no knowledge of how he had returned. He remembered only praying for deliverance and seeing an angel in the dank dungeon where he was manacled. Then he had the sensation of feathers brushing his body as he moved through space. Had it been a swan transporting him home? He gave orders then that on his death, his deliverance should be commemorated by a swan carved upon his tilting helmet, and that an effigy of his faithful dog should be placed at his feet. And now, here he lies still, in Wolverley Church as he wished, complete with swan and faithful hound.

# CHADDESLEY CORBETT

## WHO WAS ST. CASSIAN?

*Location:* 4½ miles south-east of Kidderminster.
*Map Reference:* O.S. map 139 (1:50,000); 891736.

This church is included since it is the only church in England dedicated to St. Cassian. There are various stories about St. Cassian. Some say he was an early Christian school teacher who was stabbed to death by his pagan pupils, others that he was John Cassian, Abbot of St. Victor in Marseilles in the early 5th century. It is most likely that he was in fact born in Alexandria in the 4th or 5th century, a philanthropist and missionary who lived an ascetic life, striving to keep his soul pure for God. During a European missionary pilgrimage he became Bishop of Autun in France, where he died. This Greek saint is sometimes associated with St. Nicholas, to whom the north chapel in the Chaddesley Corbet church is dedicated.

Note the scratch dial on the south chancel wall near the priest's door. Many churches bear these, but this one at Chaddesley is rare, for apart from being so clear and complete, it marks all 12 hours, denoting the lines by Roman numerals.

*CH*

# HARVINGTON

## BEHIND THESE WALLS . . .

*Location:* Along the A449 Worcester to Kidderminster Road, turning on to the A450 at Mustow Green, and then up a lane beside The Dog public house.

*Map Reference:* O.S. map 139 (1:50,000); 878745.

Harvington Hall, a Medieval and Elizabethan manor house, mostly built by Humphrey Pakington in the late 16th century, boasts the best surviving priest holes in the country. This one, which is a 'double hide' because it was secreted behind a bookcase in the library, is one of four believed to be the work of Nicholas Owen. Another is a false chimney which gave access to sufficient space under the roof to shelter as many as 40 people if necessary. Known as the master builder of hides, Owen was arrested in 1606 at Hindlip in Worcestershire, and went to his death in the Tower of London without revealing the whereabouts of the hides he had made. Harvington Hall was once a centre of Catholicism in this area, and was often visited by Saint John Wall, the last Catholic martyr in England to die for his faith in 1679. The Hall is open to the public on most days between March and October.

*CH*

# BRANSFORD

## A SNUFF MILL

*Location:* 4 miles south-west of Worcester along the A4103 to Hereford.
*Map Reference:* O.S. map 150 (1:50,000); 806532.

The Worcestershire County Council Register records this mill as being one of only two snuff mills in the county, the other being at Bewdley. It is believed that most recently it was a flour mill although now it is in a state of poor repair. The Domesday Book listed 'a mill at Bradnesford worth 20 shillings' and it is known that there were at various times two buildings on this site — a corn mill and a cloth factory. Now, however, since the course of the River Teme has been altered, what remains of the mill is landlocked in the private grounds of Bransford House, although it may be seen from the lane beside the Fox Inn.

In its snuff-making days, the mill used the waters of the Teme. Snuff, made from tobacco leaves fermented in bins, is ground after other herbs and precious oils have been added at the fermentation stage. Introduced from France during the reign of Charles II, snuff soon became popular and was considered the most polite form in which to take tobacco.

# LEIGH

## THE LARGEST FULL CRUCK BUILDING IN BRITAIN

*Location:* 5 miles from Worcester, off the A4103 to Hereford.
*Map Reference:* O.S. map 150 (1:50,000); 785534.

Of all the Tithe Barns in the country this one, recently restored by the English Heritage Trust, is now the largest full cruck building in Britain. Built in the late 13th or early 14th century by the Abbots of Pershore, it is timber framed in oak and encloses a space 141ft. by 35ft., uninterrupted by internal support. Here, as in such buildings all over England, were stored the rents or tithes paid in kind by tenants of church land (see also Elmley Castle, Bredon). The barn, standing in the grounds of Leigh Court, is still part of a working farm, but may be visited at certain times between April and October.

# LEIGH

## A LOCAL GHOST STORY

The manor of Leigh was granted by Elizabeth I to Edmund Colles whose handsome memorial lies in the church opposite. There is, however, a ghost story, well-known locally, concerning his son, also Edmund.

One Christmas Eve after his father's death, Edmund was drinking with John Leitchcroft, his friend from schooldays and now Godfather to his children, when he confessed that being bankrupt, he feared he must sell Leigh Court. John, anxious to help, rode off to Worcester to collect some of his own money.

But Edmund could not face accepting his friend's charity. Drunk now, he hid in the churchyard waiting for John's return. As Leitchcroft passed, Colles sprang out, and clutching the horse's bridle, demanded the money which hung at his friend's waist. Leitchcroft drew his sword, slashing out at his attacker, and then rode on home. Arriving in the light at the stable, he was sickened to find that a hand, severed at the wrist, still clung to the horse's bridle, but worse, one finger wore a ring which he recognised as belonging to Edmund.

Next morning Leitchcroft went to visit his friend, by now huddled in his room nursing the injured arm which he refused to let anyone tend. When they were alone John told Edmund that he knew the truth and forgave the by now abject and frightened man. The next day Edmund disappeared and was never seen alive again. Only his ghost continued to haunt Leigh at Christmas time. It is said that, driving a coach drawn by four charging horses, he careers frantically through the lanes, to take flight finally over the Tithe barn and disappear beneath the nearby waters of the River Teme.

Twelve years after Colles' death exorcism was tried in an attempt to release his troubled spirit. Twelve parsons gathered at a midnight service with an inch of candle, conjuring the ghost to rest. As the wick guttered, the lighted candle was thrown, with the ghost, into a local pond which, it is said, was then filled in.

# MALVERN

## MALVERN'S PAST IN THE PRESENT

---
*Location:* 9 miles south-west of Worcester along the A449.
*Map Reference:* O.S. map 150 (1:50,000); 772430.

---

*CH*

Malvern is one of the few places which can still supply regular employment for a lamp-lighter. Here, from the Wyche to Malvern Wells, are 93 Victorian gas lamps, erected in 1836 and still in good working order. They are maintained by a Council employee who visits them regularly, whatever the weather. He no longer has to light them each evening, for they now have time clocks fitted, but every week he goes to each one to clean it, check it for gas leaks and set the time clock. These gas lamps may not give as much light as their electric counterparts, but people like them and they help give Malvern its character and provide a touch of nostalgia.

# MALVERN

## MALVERN STATION — CAST-IRON CAPITALS

*Location:* 9 miles south-west of Worcester along the A449.
*Map Reference:* O.S. map 150 (1:50,000); 783457.

The handsome capitals in the Victorian railway station at Great Malvern are fashioned in cast-iron. Made in 1860 to support the canopy, they are perfectly maintained and are brightly painted in red, yellow and green.

*CH*

# MALVERN

## MALVERN PRIORY CHURCH: MISERICORDS

*Location:* 9 miles south-west of Worcester along the A449.
*Map Reference:* O.S. map 150 (1:50,000); 775458.

As one might expect, treasures are to be found in the Priory Church. As well as the 15th-century stained glass windows, the most complete of their period in Britain, there are the misericords and the most varied collection of 15th-century tiles in any church in England.

From the Latin 'misericordia', 'act of mercy', these seats with the narrow bracket underneath on which monks standing at service could rest, show both skill and humour in their carving. 22 of the original 24 remain and they show occupations month by month as well as legendary beasts and this witch, a symbol of the superstitious beliefs rife in the Middle Ages (see also Ripple page 42).

Decorating both sides of the Choir Screen are over 1200 tiles of about 90 different patterns, nearly all specially made here in Malvern, between 1456-1520; the only extant example of mural tiles in the country. There is also, set in a pillar opposite the door, a tile bearing an 8-line verse — perhaps the first advertisement for becoming a 'friend' of a church. Five hundred years old, it suggests the advisability of giving donations now rather than in a bequest!

*CH*

# MALVERN LINK

## A DORIC PILLAR BOX

*Location:* 6 miles from Worcester beside the A449 Worcester to Malvern Road, opposite the Common.
*Map Reference:* O.S. map 150 (1:50,000); 790482.

This rare fluted Doric pillar box, one of four erected in Malvern in December 1857, was among the first to be used in England. Made by Smith and Hawkes of the Eagle Foundry in Birmingham, this was a decided improvement on their original 1855 design. Then they made three similar prototypes, cast-iron Doric pillars (hence the name), 8ft. high, of which only one now exists. Roadside letter boxes had been used for the first time in Jersey in 1852, and came about as the result of a suggestion by a surveyor's clerk that the idea, already in use in France, might work in England. The clerk was Anthony Trollope, whose later claim to fame lay more in the pen than in the pillar box.

*CH*

83

# BIBLIOGRAPHY

County Council Register, *Worcestershire Countryside Treasures.*
Federation of W.I., *The Worcestershire Village Book.*
Gwilliam H.W., *Old Worcestershire People and Places — Vol. 1.*
Haynes C. M. and Adlam B., *Yesterday's Town, Worcester.*
Headley and Meulen Kemp, *Follies, A National Trust Guide.*
Lawrence-Smith K., *Tales of Old Worcestershire.*
Leatherbarrow J.S., *Worcestershire.*
Lloyd, the Rev. R. H., *Bredon Hill and its Villages.*
Mee A., *The King's England — Worcesteshire.*
Pevsner N., *Worcestershire.*
Salter M., *The Old Parish Churches of Worcestershire.*

# INDEX

# NOTES